# Magic Tricks to make and do

## Ben Denne

### Designed by Russell Punter
### Illustrated by Andi Good

Photographs by Howard Allman
Edited by Gillian Doherty
Cover design by Michelle Lawrence

Cards © by Piatnik, Vienna

# Contents

DISCARD

Q. How do you make your audience leave after the show?
A. Tell them the terrible jokes in this book.

# Making a wand

You will need:
A piece of black paper
A piece of white paper
A glue stick
Two pencils

You could use purple or gold paper to make your wand.

1. Cut out a piece of black paper, about the same size as this page. Roll it up tightly around two pencils.

Put glue along here.

2. When you have rolled up all the paper, unroll it a little and put some glue along the edge. Then roll it up again.

Press on the wand with both hands.

3. Hold the wand down firmly for about a minute, until the glue dries. Make sure you hold it with the glued edge underneath.

Use some of the stickers in this book to brighten up your wand.

The strips help the wand to keep its shape.

4. Cut out two thin strips of white paper. Cover one side of them with glue. Wrap them around the ends of the wand.

5. Hold your wand with one end facing the floor. Shake it until the pencils fall out. Now you're ready to do some magic.

Q. What do you call a magician in a spaceship?
A. A flying sorcerer!

# The incredible shrinking wand

## Getting ready

1. Cut out two strips of white paper. They should be wide enough to cover the strips on the ends of your wand.

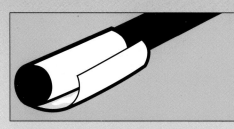

2. Roll a strip around one end of your wand. Unroll it a little, put some glue along the edge and roll it up again quite loosely.

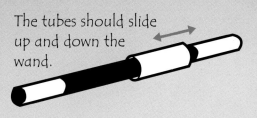

The tubes should slide up and down the wand.

3. Do the same with the other end of your wand. The tubes should fit well, but be loose enough to slide along the wand.

## Doing the trick

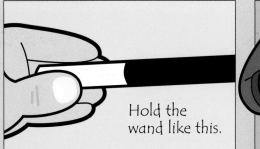

Hold the wand like this.

1. Hold the tubes between your middle finger and thumb. Cover the front with your fingers.

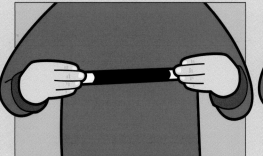

2. Close your fingers, so people can't see between them. Then say that you can make your wand change size.

Keep the ends of the wand covered with your hands.

3. Look like you are really concentrating. Then slowly bring your hands together, so the tubes slide along the wand.

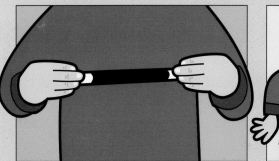

4. Say you can make the wand grow again. Slowly pull your hands apart, so the tubes slide back out along the wand.

If anyone asks to look at the wand, say it is very dangerous for non-magicians to touch it!

5. Take a bow. Then, put your wand away before anyone can see it. Continue your show with a normal wand.

Q. Which book do magicians like best?
A. Alice in Wand-erland.

3

# Finger in a matchbox

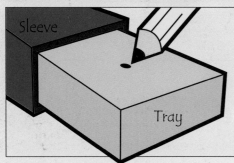

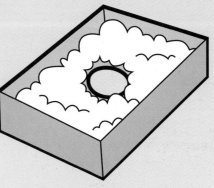

You will need:
An empty matchbox
A pencil
A pair of scissors
A cotton ball
A glue stick
A paintbrush
Red food dye, or red poster paint

## Getting ready

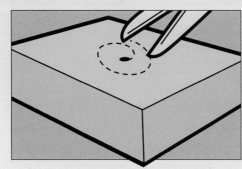

1. Slide the sleeve off the matchbox. Poke a small hole in the bottom of the matchbox tray with a pencil.

2. Cut around the hole, making it a little bigger. Keep making it bigger, until your middle finger just fits through it.

3. Put glue around the hole. Pull a cotton ball apart and press the cotton onto the glue. Be careful not to cover the hole.

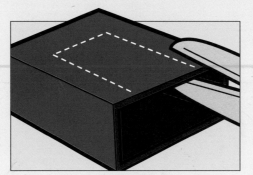

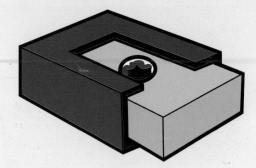

4. Dip a paintbrush into some red food dye or poster paint. Dab a small amount onto the cotton around the hole.

5. Cut a rectangle out of the bottom of one end of the matchbox sleeve. Make it wide enough for your finger to fit through.

6. Slide the sleeve onto the matchbox tray, so that the cutout part of the sleeve is over the hole in the tray.

4

Q. Why are fingers reliable?
A. Because you can count on them.

# Doing the trick

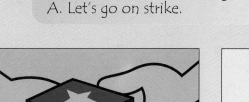

Q. What did one match say to the other?
A. Let's go on strike.

1. Hold your hand out, with your palm facing up. Put the matchbox on it, with the cutout part underneath, like this.

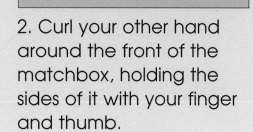

2. Curl your other hand around the front of the matchbox, holding the sides of it with your finger and thumb.

3. Show your audience the closed matchbox. Tell them you have something special inside it that you want to show them.

4. Put your middle finger through the hole in the tray, then open the sleeve. Try this beforehand, until you can do it smoothly.

YUCK!

ERRGH!

5. Show your audience the matchbox with your finger inside. Make sure you keep the front covered with your other hand.

6. Pause for a few seconds, then wiggle your finger around in the matchbox. This should really make your audience scream!

Here are some ideas for how to decorate your matchbox.

# A ready-sliced banana

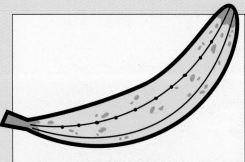

You will need:
A banana
A clean sewing needle
A magic wand

## Getting ready

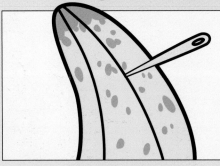

1. Take a banana. A slightly brown or freckled one works best. Poke a needle into it along an edge near one end.

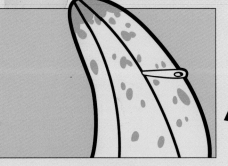

2. Push the needle through the banana but not through the skin on the other side. Wiggle it from side to side and pull it out.

3. Repeat step 2 until you have made ten tiny holes along the banana. Make the holes an equal distance apart.

## Doing the trick

1. Tell your audience you can control the banana with your wand. Say you will command the banana to cut itself into slices.

2. Hold the banana up and point your wand at it. Say some magic words and stare very hard at the banana.

3. Unpeel the banana. It will be in slices. To end the trick, eat a slice of banana and offer the rest to your audience.

Q. Why are bananas never lonely?
A. Because they hang around in bunches.

# The unburstable balloon

## Getting ready

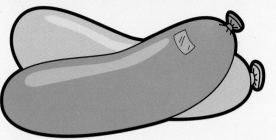

Blow up two balloons and tie the ends. Press a small piece of tape onto one of the balloons.

## Doing the trick

1. Tell your audience that you can make a balloon unburstable. Then give somebody the balloon without any tape on it.

2. Challenge the volunteer to stick a knitting needle into the balloon without bursting it. Then get ready for a loud bang.

3. Hold the other balloon with the tape facing you. Carefully poke the knitting needle through the tape. The balloon won't burst.

4. Take out the needle. Then hide the balloon. It won't burst even when you take out the needle, but it will start to go down.

Q. What sort of music do balloons listen to?
A. Pop.

# Counting cards

## Getting ready

1. A pack of cards is called a deck. Look through a deck of cards and take out a joker, an ace (with an A on it) and one of each number from 2 to 10.

2. Put the cards on a table, face up in a line. They should be in this order from left to right: 6, 5, 4, 3, 2, ace, joker, 10, 9, 8, 7.

3. Keeping the cards in order, gather them up and place them face down. Keep the 6 on top and the 7 on the bottom.

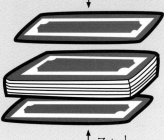

↓ 6 is here.

↑ 7 is here.

There is no card with the number 1 on it. An ace is the same as number 1.

Q. How do playing cards walk?
A. They shuffle.

# Doing the trick

6 is here.  7 is here.

✗

You are here.

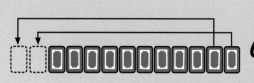

The person moving the cards can move up to 10 cards.

1. Deal the cards out. Place them face down in front of you, with the 6 on the left and the 7 on the right.

2. Turn away. Then ask someone to move cards one by one from the right end to the left, but not to tell you how many.

3. Turn back. Say you will ask the cards how many were moved. Wave your wand around over the cards.

Seventh card

4. Turn over the seventh card from the left. The number on it will be the same as the number of cards the person moved.

5. If the card you turn over is the ace, it means that only one card was moved. If it's the joker, then no cards were moved.

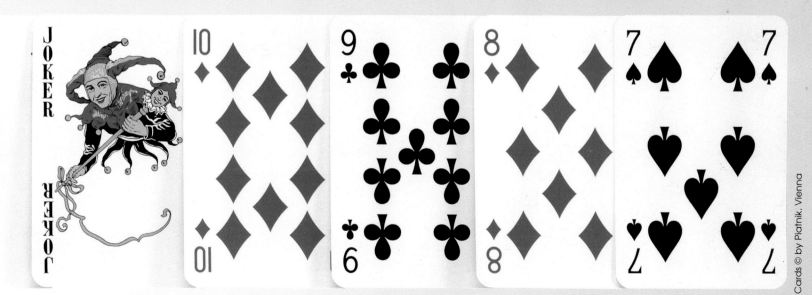

Q. Where do sailors play cards?
A. On the deck.

9

Cards © by Piatnik, Vienna

# Self-joining paperclips

It is difficult to see why this trick works, but it always does.

You will need:
Two paperclips
A strip of paper

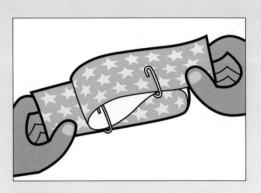

Big loop of paperclip

1. Take a strip of paper. Bend a third of it over on itself (but don't fold it). Clip a paperclip on, with the big loop facing you.

2. Now bend the other third of paper back on itself, to make an S-shape. Clip it, with the big loop of the paperclip facing you.

3. Hold the ends of the strip of paper and slowly pull them apart. The paperclips will move closer to each other.

4. When the paperclips are touching each other, pull sharply. They will jump off the strip of paper and join together.

Q. Why do paperclips date notepaper?
A. Because they're attached to each other.

# Changing cards

You will need:
A deck of cards
Poster tack
A paperclip

This is more of a puzzle than a trick, but it fools everybody.

Cards © by Piatnik, Vienna

Put poster tack on all but one card.

1. Take a joker and four other cards from a deck. Put a ball of poster tack on the backs of four of them, including the joker.

There is no poster tack on this card.

2. Stick the cards together, like this. Put the card without poster tack on at the back and the joker in the middle.

3. Now show the cards to your audience. Tell them to look carefully at where the joker is. Then turn the cards over.

4. Challenge a volunteer from the audience to clip a paper clip over the joker, without turning the cards over.

5. Your volunteer will probably clip the middle card. Turn the cards over and see where the clip really is.

Q. What happens at a card school?
A. People learn a great deal.

# Moving matchbox

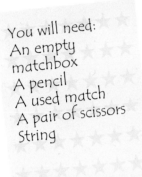

You will need:
An empty matchbox
A pencil
A used match
A pair of scissors
String

## Getting ready

Make holes in the short sides of the tray, at the bottom.

1. Take the tray out of an empty matchbox. Use a sharp pencil to make a small hole at each end of the tray.

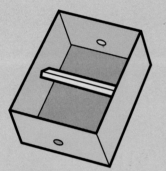

2. Trim a used match with scissors to make it just bigger than the width of the tray. Wedge it across the inside of the tray.

3. Thread a long piece of string through the holes in the tray and over the match. Then put the sleeve back on the box.

## Doing the trick

Start with the matchbox at the top.

1. Push the matchbox to one end of the string. Pull the string to stretch it tight. Hold it up vertically with the box at the top.

2. Tell the audience that you can control the matchbox. Ask a volunteer to say the commands "go" and "stop".

3. Relax the string to make the matchbox move. To stop it, stretch the string tight. Make it move at the volunteer's command.

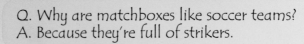
Q. Why are matchboxes like soccer teams?
A. Because they're full of strikers.

# Escaped prisoner

You could draw your own prisoner, or use the sticker in this book.

You will need:
A piece of paper
A pair of scissors
A pencil
A glue stick
String

## Getting ready

1. Cut out two rectangles of paper, about the size of a playing card. Make them exactly the same size.

2. Draw straight lines down one piece of paper. Draw a picture of a man on the other (or use the prisoner sticker in this book).

3. Cover the back of one piece of paper in glue. Put a piece of string about the width of this page across the middle of it.

## Doing the trick

4. Press the back of the other piece of paper on top, so it completely covers the first piece. Leave it to dry.

1. Show the audience both sides of the sign. Say the man is an escaped prisoner and you are going to recapture him.

When you spin the sign, it will look like the man is behind bars.

2. Hold the ends of the string, so the man is upside down, facing you. Then spin it quickly between your fingers and thumbs.

Q. How did the female prisoner escape from jail?
A. She used the ladder in her stockings.

# Coin drop

You will need:
A piece of paper
A small coin
A slightly bigger coin
A pencil

1. You can prepare this trick while the audience is watching. Put a small coin on a piece of paper and draw around it.

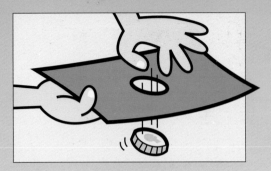

2. Cut out the circle you have drawn. Then hold up the piece of paper and drop the small coin through the hole.

3. Now challenge a volunteer from the audience to fit the bigger coin through the hole. It seems impossible.

4. Take the paper and the coin back. Fold the paper in half, so the fold is across the middle of the hole. Put the big coin in it, like this.

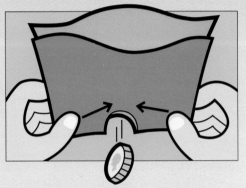

5. Hold the folded piece of paper at the bottom. push the sides up and into the middle. The coin will fall through.

Any two round coins will work for this trick, as long as one is slightly bigger than the other.

Q. Why is money called dough?
A. Because we knead it.

# Magic paper

## Getting ready

Make two rips in a small piece of paper, from the top to a third of the way down. Fold down the part between the rips.

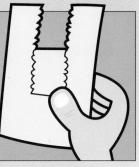

The two rips should be exactly the same length.

Use bright or patterned paper to make this trick look more flashy.

## Doing the trick

Hold the paper between your fingers and thumb.

1. Face your audience. Hold the paper up in your right hand, with the folded part facing you, and your thumb over it.

Pretend you are holding two threads.

2. Hold up your left hand behind the paper. Say you are holding invisible threads attached to the sticking-up parts.

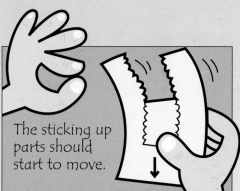

The sticking up parts should start to move.

3. Slowly pull your left hand away from the paper, as if holding the strings. At the same time, slide your right thumb down.

This looks best if you do it slowly.

4. Look like you are really concentrating. Move your left hand forward again and push your right thumb back up.

Q. Why is paper like a piano?
A. You can make notes on it.

# Wobbly wand

Ibbedy-zibbedy squiggledy pop!

The quicker you shake, the bendier your wand looks.

1. Hold out your wand for your audience to examine. Tell them that you can turn it into a bendy wand by saying some magic words.

2. Hold your wand loosely at one end, between your first finger and thumb. Look at your wand and say some magic words.

3. Now move your hand quickly up and down. Make quite small movements. Your wand will look as if it's bending.

# Knotty problem

Use a piece of string about twice the height of this page.

1. Ask a volunteer to hold the ends of a piece of string and tie a knot in it without letting go of the ends. It seems impossible.

2. When he gives up, lay the string on the table. Cross your arms. Pick up the ends of the string, one end at a time.

3. Now uncross your arms without letting go of the ends of the string. A knot will magically appear in the middle of it.

Q. Why can't magicians stay in one place?
A. Because they're always wand-ering around.

# Magic matchbox

You will need:
An empty matchbox
A pair of scissors
A pencil
A piece of thin white cardboard

In this trick, a picture magically appears in an empty matchbox.

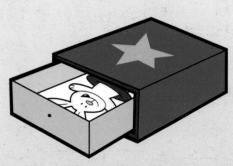

## Getting ready

1. Take the tray out of an empty matchbox. Cut a piece off the end of the tray, about a third of the way along it.

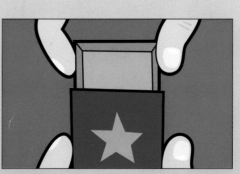

The mark will tell you which is the long part of the tray.

2. Put both parts of the tray back in the sleeve, with the long part sticking out slightly. Make a mark on the end of the long part.

3. Cut out a piece of cardboard small enough to fit into the tray. Draw a picture on it, or put a sticker on it. Put it in the tray.

## Doing the trick

1. Hold the matchbox vertically, with the long part of the tray at the top. Tell the audience that it is a magic matchbox.

2. Pull up the long part of the tray. The picture will stay hidden inside the matchbox, so it will look as if the tray is empty.

3. Close the box. Tap it with your wand. Then push the short part of the tray up from underneath, like this. The picture will appear.

Q. What did the matchbox say to the used match?
A. You're fired!

# Disappearing coin

## Getting ready

1. Turn the plastic cup upside down on a piece of cardboard. Hold it steady and carefully draw around it with a pencil.

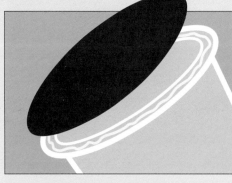

2. Cut out the circle of cardboard. Put a thin layer of glue around the rim of the cup. Press the cardboard onto it.

3. Let the glue dry. Then carefully cut off any cardboard sticking out around the rim of the cup. Wipe off any extra glue too.

*Never let your audience see underneath the cup.*

4. Roll some paper into a tube. Make the tube just wide enough to fit over the cup. Glue the edges together. Leave it to dry.

Q. Where do frogs keep their money?
A. At the riverbank.

# Doing the trick

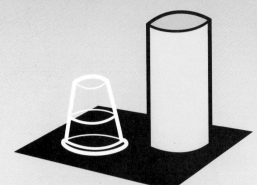

1. Put the cup and tube next to each other on the cardboard, like this. Ask your audience for a coin. A thin one works best.

Make sure the tube covers the cup.

2. Put the coin on the cardboard and say that you are going to make it disappear. Then slide the paper tube over the cup.

3. Squeeze the tube between your fingers and thumb, so it grips the cup. Lift them both up and put them on top of the coin.

4. Now lift the tube all the way off, leaving the cup where it is. It will look as if the coin has disappeared.

5. Put the tube over the cup and tap it with your wand. Lift them both off to make the coin reappear.

You could make the tube with shiny paper to distract the audience's attention from the cup.

Q. What do you call a very rich rabbit?
A. A million-hare.

**19**

# Magic handkerchief

In this trick, you push a wand straight through a handkerchief.

This trick works best if you use a big handkerchief.

1. Show your audience a handkerchief, to prove that there are no holes in it. Tell them you can push your wand through it.

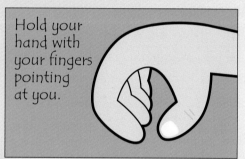

Hold your hand with your fingers pointing at you.

2. Make a circle with the first finger and thumb of your right hand, but leave a gap between them. Put the handkerchief over it.

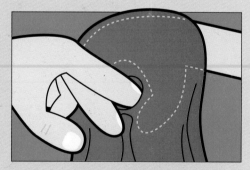

3. Push the first finger of your left hand into the circle. Bring your middle finger in through the gap, to make a tunnel.

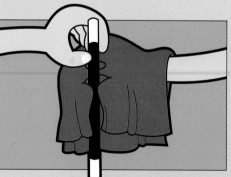

4. Now push your wand through the tunnel. It will look as if your wand is going straight through the handkerchief.

5. Shake the handkerchief out and show it to the audience, so they can see that there are still no holes in it.

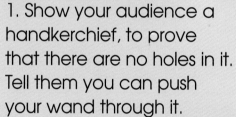

Q. Why couldn't the viper viper nose?
A. Because the adder adder handkerchief!

# Jumping rubber band

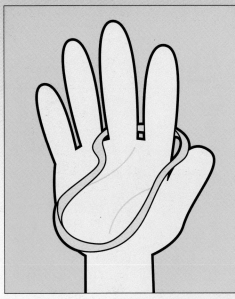

1. Put a rubber band over your first and middle fingers. Hold it up like this, so the back of your hand faces the audience.

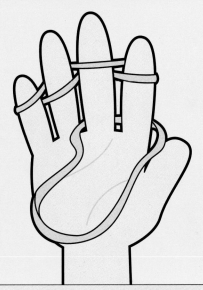

2. On the same hand, twist another rubber band around the tops of your fingers. Do this while the audience watches.

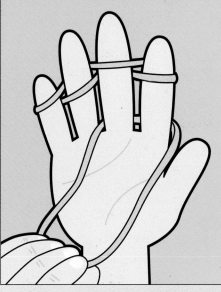

3. Now take the first rubber band between your fingers and thumb. Stretch it back quite far, like this.

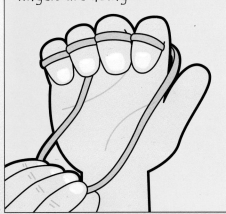

The back of your hand should always face the audience, so they can't see what your fingers are doing.

4. With the rubber band stretched back, curl your fingers over to make a fist. Let the rubber band go and straighten your fingers.

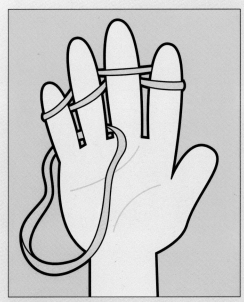

5. The band will magically jump across the barrier made by the second rubber band, onto your other two fingers.

If you do this trick quickly, it looks really impressive.

Q. Have you heard the one about the rubber band?
A. They could play anything at a stretch!

# Find the card

## Getting ready

1. Look through a deck of cards. Some of the numbers and letters have rounded tops and some of them don't.

Not rounded tops

Rounded tops

Count the tens as cards with rounded tops, even though the one isn't rounded.

Hold the cards with one pile just in front of the other, to keep them separate.

2. Place all the cards with rounded tops in a pile and all the other cards in another pile. Place the piles together, like this.

Cards © by Piatnik, Vienna

## Doing the trick

Separate the cards smoothly, so nobody knows that you have arranged them before.

1. Ask for two volunteers. Give the cards with rounded numbers to one of them and the other cards to the other.

2. Ask your volunteers to pick a card each and memorize it. They mustn't show you the cards they pick.

3. Ask them to swap the two cards they picked. Then ask them to put the new card anywhere in their part of the deck.

22

Q. Why did the thief steal the deck of cards?
A. Because it was full of diamonds.

In this group of cards, this card is the odd one out.

4. Take both piles of cards back. Put them together, without mixing them up, and fan them out in front of you.

5. Go through the cards with rounded tops looking for one without a rounded top. Do the opposite with the other pile of cards.

6. The two cards that you pick out will be the cards that your volunteers chose. Show them and take a bow.

# Magic knot

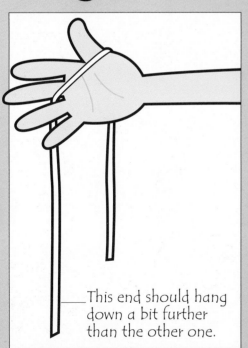

This end should hang down a bit further than the other one.

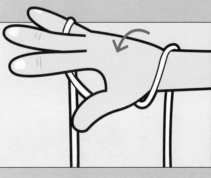

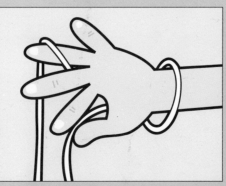

1. Cut a piece of string, about twice the length of this page. Lay it over your right hand, like this.

2. Angle your hand forward. Take the shorter end of the string between your finger and thumb.

3. Still holding the string, shake your hand, so the string falls off. A knot will appear.

Q. Why are cards like businessmen?
A. They come in suits.

# Abracadabra magic cards

1. Deal a row of three cards onto a table. Deal them out from left to right, facing up so your audience can see them.

2. Deal three more cards from left to right, just under the first three. Keep doing this until you have three columns of seven cards.

3. Ask a volunteer from the audience to memorize one of the cards on the table, but not to tell you which one.

Lay out the three columns of cards like this.

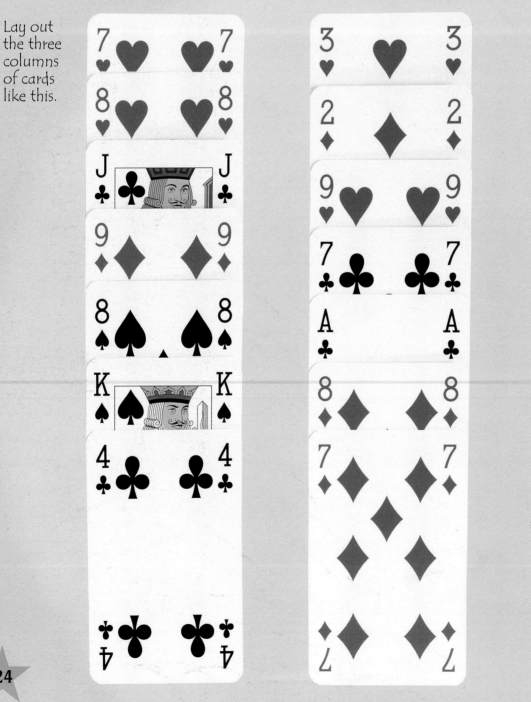

4. Ask your volunteer to say which column the card is in. Then gather each column up, so you have three piles.

5. Put the three piles of cards together, with the pile that contains your volunteer's card in the middle.

6. Deal out three columns of cards in exactly the same way, and repeat steps 4 and 5. Then do this step again.

7. Now tell the audience that "abracadabra" is a very magic word. Say that you are about to prove it.

8. Take a card from the top of the pile. Put it face down on the table. As you do this, say "a": the first letter of "abracadabra".

9. Now do the same thing with the next card in the pile, and say "b". Lay it face down, on top of the first card.

10. Keep putting cards down one by one on the table. Each time you put one down, say the next letter of "abracadabra".

11. When you get to the last "a", put the card face up on the table. It will be the card your volunteer chose.

Q. What card game do alligators like best?
A. Snap, of course!

# Card control

1. Hold a deck of cards up with the backs facing the audience. Tell them you need a volunteer for a mind control trick.

2. As you do step 1, secretly memorize the card that is facing you. Then put the deck of cards face down on the table.

Bottom card

3. Mess up all the cards on the table, like this. Do it so the bottom card ends up slightly separate and remember where it is.

4. Say you will ask the volunteer to pick a certain card and that you will control her mind to guide her to the right one.

5. Ask the volunteer to pick the card you memorized. For example, if it was the two of spades, say, "Point to the two of spades."

6. Ask the volunteer to give you the card without looking at it. Look at the new card, memorize it and put it to one side.

Q. What do magicians wear to keep warm?
A. Card-igans.

7. Now ask for the card that your volunteer just gave you. She won't know she has already picked it.

8. Once again, look at the card and memorize it, then put it with the other card your volunteer chose.

9. Ask for the card your volunteer just gave you, but when she chooses one, shake your head and tell her to try again.

10. When she chooses another one, tell her she is wrong again. Say you will pick it. Pick up the card you memorized in step 3.

Cards © by Piatnik, Vienna

11. Pick up the three cards. Lay them in a line face down on the table, then turn them over. The audience will be amazed.

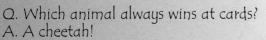

Q. Which animal always wins at cards?
A. A cheetah!

# Jumping coin

1. Ask your audience for two coins. The coins don't need to be the same.

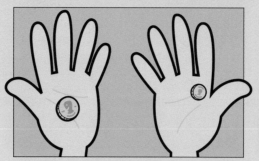

2. Put one coin in the middle of your left palm and the other on the right side of your right palm.

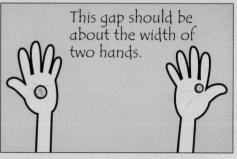

This gap should be about the width of two hands.

3. Lay your hands on the table with a gap between them and your palms facing up.

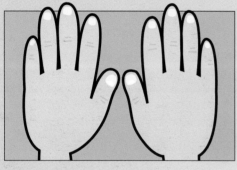

4. Turn your hands over quickly with the coins on them, like this. The coin on your right hand will jump across to your left hand.

5. Ask the audience where the coins are. When they tell you there is one under each hand, lift your hands up and show them.

# Changing coins

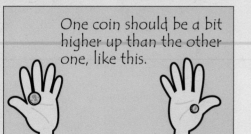

One coin should be a bit higher up than the other one, like this.

1. For another version of the jumping coin trick, put two different coins on the sides of your palms.

2. Tell the audience to look closely at which coin is in which hand. Then do steps 3 and 4 of "Jumping coin".

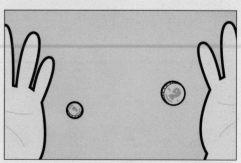

3. Ask the audience which coin is under which hand, then lift your hands. They will have swapped places.

Q. What happened when the cat swallowed a coin?
A. There was money in the kitty!

# One-sided paper

You will need:
A strip of paper about the width of a matchbox and about twice as long as this page (Giftwrap or newspaper work well.)
A pen
Clear sticky tape

In this trick, you turn a normal strip of paper into a loop with only one side.

1. Hold up the strip of paper and tell your audience that it only has one side. If they laugh, say you will prove it.

Twist the paper over once, like this.

2. Hold the strip up like this, to make a loop. Twist one of the ends over once, to make a single twist in the loop.

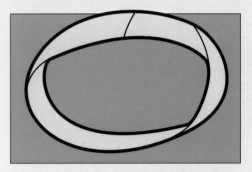

3. Hold the ends of the loop together and stick them with tape. Then ask for a volunteer from the audience.

4. Ask the volunteer to draw a line along the middle of the strip, without taking the pen off the paper.

5. Eventually, the line will join up with itself. Point out that the pen has never left the paper, so the paper must be one-sided.

Q. What's the angriest part of a newspaper?
A. The crossword!

# Loopy loops

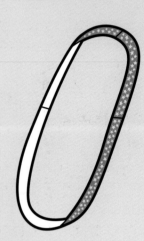

## Getting ready

You will need:
Lots of long strips of paper, about the width of a matchbox (Giftwrap or newspaper works well.)
Scissors
Clear sticky tape

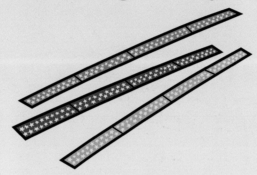

1. Stick strips of paper together with tape until you have a strip about 1.5m (5ft) long. Make three of these long strips.

2. Use the first strip to make a big loop without any twists in it. Hold the ends together and stick them with tape.

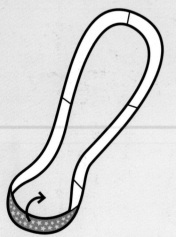

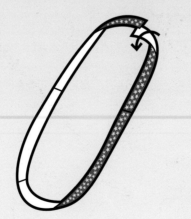

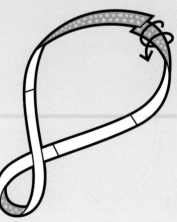

3. Take the bottom of the loop and carefully turn it over once, like this, so that part of it is twisted.

4. Pick up another strip. Make it into a loop. Turn one of the ends over, like this, and stick the ends together with tape.

5. Pick up the third strip and make a loop. Turn one end over twice, like this. Then stick the ends together with tape.

Q. What's black and white and read all over?
A. A newspaper.

# Doing the trick

1. Show the three loops of paper to the audience. Put the last two loops you made on one side and hold up the first one.

2. Cut the loop in half lengthways, like this. Hold up the two separate thin loops, to show the audience.

3. Put the two thin loops on one side and pick up the second loop you made. Ask for a volunteer from the audience.

4. Challenge the volunteer to make two loops by cutting the loop in half. In fact, it will end up as one enormous loop.

5. Now ask the volunteer to try again, using the third loop. Say that you will use your wand to help her.

6. Wave your wand around over the loop. This time, your volunteer will end up with two loops joined together.

Q. What's black and white and red all over?
A. A penguin with sunburn.

# Putting on a show

When putting on a show, it looks much better if you have a box to keep your tricks in. Make one by decorating a large cardboard box. Tape a piece of cardboard across the middle of it, to make two compartments.

Start your show by putting all of your tricks in one compartment.

When you've done a trick, put it into the other compartment.

Do all your tricks with your audience standing in front of you, so they can't see how they are done.

If you don't want the audience to look closely at something, wave your wand to distract them.

Cards © by Piatnik, Vienna

p.14 photograph © Powerstock

First published in 2007 by Usborne Publishing Ltd. Usborne House, 83-85 Saffron Hill, London EC1N 8RT, England. www.usborne.com